YOUR KNOWLEDGE HAS VALUE

- We will publish your bachelor's and master's thesis, essays and papers

- Your own eBook and book - sold worldwide in all relevant shops

- Earn money with each sale

Upload your text at www.GRIN.com
and publish for free

General Facts, History and Present of the British Royal Family

Anne Sander

Bibliographic information published by the German National Library:

The German National Library lists this publication in the National Bibliography; detailed bibliographic data are available on the Internet at http://dnb.dnb.de.

ISBN: 9783668665958
This book is also available as an ebook.

© GRIN Publishing GmbH
Nymphenburger Straße 86
80636 München

All rights reserved

Print and binding: Books on Demand GmbH, Norderstedt, Germany
Printed on acid-free paper from responsible sources.

The present work has been carefully prepared. Nevertheless, authors and publishers do not incur liability for the correctness of information, notes, links and advice as well as any printing errors.

GRIN web shop: https://www.grin.com/document/416288

The Royal Family
A brief summary

Overview:

1. General Facts 3
   - Role: 3
   - Coronation: 3
   - The Royal Coat of Arms and motto: 4
2. History 4
   - Offa: 4
   - King William I: 4
   - King Henry VIII: 4
3. Present 6
   Queen Elizabeth II: 6
   - Royal Children: 7
   - Royal Grandchildren: 8
   - The Royal Wedding: 8
   Sources: 9

1. General Facts

Role:

The Royal Family has to make sure that there is a strong unity within Great Britain. Every member of the Royal Family is able to participate in every event in the UK, such as openings of new buildings, acts of commemoration or the Olympic Games this summer. Today the head of the Royal Family nearly has no political power, but has more of a representative role. Furthermore the Queen is the Head of the Armed Forces. With that function she is the only one who can decide whether the country is at war or when the war is finished. Every British Monarch is Head of the Church of England which comprises the appointment of bishops. Every priest has to swear an oath not on the Pope like the Catholics or on God like Protestant priests, but on the Queen herself.

Coronation:

Usually a coronation of a British Monarch takes place after a few months of the previous king or queen. It is a happy ceremony and it would be out of place to be in a time of mourning for the late monarch. Westminster Abbey is the place where the coronations are being hold. It contains King Edward's chair, an old wooden chair and a stone which is placed underneath it which are a traditional part of a coronation ceremony. The stone actually belongs to Scotland and is hold at Edinburgh Castle. To every coronation it is brought to London and right after the ceremony the stone is taken back to Scotland. The coronation is performed by an Archbishop of Canterbury. It is an important ritual where a lot of guests including international politicians appear.

The typical type of clothing is a crimson surcoat, Parliament robe, a tunic and accessories like a gold scarf. Throughout the coronation the archbishop walks in all four corners of the church and has to ask "Sirs, I here present unto you ..., your undoubted King. Wherefore all you who are come this day to do your homage and service, are you willing to do the same?" After the approval of the people the monarch has to swear an oath. After the oath the king or queen is rubbed with ointment and the crown jewels are delivered to him by the archbishop. He gets the orb, two scepters and at last the crown is placed on his or her head.

The Royal Coat of Arms and motto:

The shield is being hold by the English Lion on the left side. On the other side it is supported by the Scottish Unicorn. The unicorn is tethered because in earlier times a free unicorn was judged as a very dangerous and wild creature. The words "Dieu et mon droit" are engraved on the crest. It is French for "God and my right". It was introduced and first used by Richard the Lionheart. It is used by the Queen and in court rooms. It is seen on many government documents, forms and also passports.

2. History

Offa:

The beginnings of the Royal Family date back to 757 AD. The first king to be known was King Offa, who reigned from 757-796 AD. He was a Viking and the first Anglo-Saxon who called himself King of England. His territory included Kent, Sussex, East Anglia and the Midlands.

King William I:

Another important King was William I. also called William the Conqueror. In 1066 he killed King Harold II, who was the current King of England at that time, making William the new king. His most significant achievements were the construction of the Tower of England in 1078 and the Norman Cathedral at Winchester a year later. It is one of the oldest gothic churches in England. William died in 1087 of injuries after falling from his horse and with his death his reign ended.

King Henry VIII:

Henry VIII is one of the best known kings of England, especially because of his six wives. He was the second monarch of the House of Tudors. Henry was born in 1491 and died in 1547 at the age of 56. His father died in 1509 and he was made the new King of England. His first wife was Catherine of Aragon who he married in 1509. Their daughter Mary was born in 1516 and later became Mary I of England, the Bloody Mary. Still being married to Catherine of Aragon he met Anne Boleyn. Fascinated by her beauty and intelligence Henry grew interested in her. After 18 years of marriage, Henry wanted a divorce. He asked for permission to do so from the Pope, but his request was denied. As a result he started to abandon the Church of Rome and made himself head of the Church of England so it was under his control and not Rome's.

In 1533 a new archbishop, Thomas Cranmer, annuls Henry's marriage with Catherine. The same year he marries Anne Boleyn. She was then crowned to be Queen Consort. Short time after their marriage Anne was pregnant with a child presumed to be male, but it turned out to be a girl. On the 7th September 1533 Elizabeth Tudor was born. She later became Elizabeth I, Queen of England. Now Henry had two daughters and still no male heir. Anne feared her daughter's position being endangered by Mary, Henry's now bastard daughter. That is why he sent Elizabeth to the countryside. Catherine of Aragon died on 7th January 1536 and Anne was pregnant again. She knew that if she gave birth to a girl again it would be a danger to her position as Queen of England. Now that Catherine was dead, Henry could easily divorce Anne and marry again. He started seeing Jane Seymour, the great-great-granddaughter of King Edward III, which made her King Henry's fifth cousin. After nearly four months of pregnancy, Anne gave birth to a dead foetus. Losing his final interest in his wife, Henry declared that his marriage with Anne invalid. To get rid of her she was accused of treason and having an incestuous relationship with her brother. Anne Boleyn was executed on 19th May 1536 at the age of 35. Henry married Jane Seymour only eleven days after Anne's execution. In contrast to her, Jane gave birth to a son. In early 1537 she became pregnant and in October that year, Edward VI of England was born. His christening was three days later. The king's two daughters were present, his mother however was missing. Jane's labour had been long and difficult and she died two weeks after giving birth. Henry called Jane Seymour his only real wife and even was buried next to her. The only real reason for this is that she was the one who gave him a much wanted male heir.

After her death a new queen was needed and on 6th January 1540 King Henry married Anne of Cleves. She was a German noblewoman, born in Düsseldorf in September 1515. After six months the marriage was being annulled again, on the grounds that their marriage was not fulfilled. Anne wasn't offended by this and gladly agreed to their divorce. They had no interest in each other and Henry married her just for the sake of having a wife and queen.

Almost immediately after this annulment Henry married Catherine Howard, the cousin of Anne Boleyn. At that time Henry was nearly fifty years old and only had one son. His new wife was thirty years younger than him. In spring 1541 Catherine had an affair with her old lover, who was one of the king's servants. Their affair was exposed and Catherine was charged with treason and adultery. Her execution was on 13th February 1542. Henry's last wife was Catherine Parr. He married her in July 1543. Her mother was a close friend and also servant of Henry's first wife Catherine of Aragon. After three and a half years of marriage with Catherine Parr, King Henry died on 28th January 1547. All in all he had six wives. There is an easy mnemonic for their fates. Divorced, beheaded, died, divorced, beheaded, survived.

3. Present

Queen Elizabeth II:

Elizabeth Alexandra Mary was born on 21st April 1926. Her official title is Elizabeth II, by the Grace of God, of the United Kingdom of Great Britain and Northern Ireland and of her other realms and territories Queen, Head of the Commonwealth, Defender of the Faith. She was crowned at the age of 25 and still is the head of the Royal Family. Elizabeth is the first Queen since 1707. She is the granddaughter of King George V. Her parents are King George VI and Elizabeth Bowes-Lyon. She was educated at home together with her younger sister Margaret. They studied arts and music. Also they were taught in horseback riding and became good swimmers.

In 1936 her grandfather died and her uncle Edward VIII became king. However he gave up the throne and his younger brother, George VI, Elizabeth's father, became the new king. This made Elizabeth the next claimant to the throne at the age of 10. On 20th November 1947 Princess Elizabeth married Prince Phillip, Duke of Edinburgh. They have four children. The oldest is Prince Charles who was born on 14th November 1948. He has two younger brothers and a younger sister. In January 1952 Elizabeth and her husband Philip were on a trip to Australia. During their trip Elizabeth's father King George VI died. She was then automatically Queen Elizabeth

II. She instantly flew back home and was crowned on 2nd June 1953 being 25 years old. She is not only the Queen of England, Scotland and Northern Ireland, but also of Canada, New Zealand, Arkotiri and Dhekelia, Anguilla, Bermuda, British Antarctic Territory, British Indian Ocean Territory, British Virgin Islands, Cayman Islands, Falkland Islands, Gibraltar, Montserrat, Pitcairn Islands, Saint Helena, Ascension and Tristan da Cunha, South Georgia and the South Sandwich Islands and the Turks and Caicos Islands. Almost all of the flags of the territories contain a small Union Jack to show their affiliation to the United Kingdom. In February 2012 she celebrated her Diamond Jubilee, signalizing her 60 years as Queen of England. It was celebrated throughout the country. She now is the second longest reigning Queen after Queen Victoria. She was queen for 63 years. This means Queen Elizabeth must stay queen until 2015. If the Queen decides to abdicate, retires or dies Prince Charles is the new king of England. The next heirs to the throne are Prince William and his brother Prince Harry. Additionally, she opened the Olympic Games 2012 with a short film, in which she and Daniel Craig starred. Elizabeth played herself and Daniel Craig personified James Bond. Most of the time the Queen lives in Buckingham Palace in London but she also has castles in areas all over the United Kingdom like Windsor Castle or Balmoral Castle in Scotland.

Royal Children:

All four children were born in Buckingham Palace, London. Prince Charles, Prince of Wales was born in 1948. Because he is the first born he is the best known and also the next person to be king. He married Diana Spencer in 1981. Unfortunately she died in a car crash in 1997. His next wife was Camilla Parker Bowles, who he married in 2005. Princess Anne, Princess Royal was born 1950 and married Mark Phillips in 1973, however they got divorced in 1989. In 1992 she married Timothy Laurence. Prince Andrew, Duke of York was born in 1960 and married Sarah Ferguson in 1986. Prince Edward was born in 1964 as the youngest of the four Royal Children. He married Sophie Rhys-Jones in 1999.

Royal Grandchildren:

The Queen has eight grandchildren. Prince William and his brother Prince Harry were born in 1982 and 1984. They are the children of Prince Charles and Lady Diana Spencer. Like their father they're the best known of their generation. Prince William not only because him being one of the next claimants to the throne but also because of his wedding in 2011. His brother is also quite famous, although for scandals like him wearing a Swastika armband. Princess Anne and Mark Phillips also had two children, Peter and Zara Phillips who were born in 1977 and 1981. Prince Andrew has two daughters with his wife Sarah Ferguson, Princess Beatrice of York who was born in 1988 and Princess Eugenie who is two years younger than her sister. The youngest of the Queen's grandchildren are Lady Louise Windsor and James Windsor, children of Prince Edward and Sophie Rhys-Jones. They were born in 2003 and 2007. At the time of their parents' wedding it was decided, with the couple's agreement, that any children they had should not be given the name Royal Highness, but a title as son or daughter of an Earl.

The Royal Wedding:

On Friday, 29th April 2011 Prince William, son of Prince Charles and Princess Diane, married Catherine (Kate) Middleton. Their relationship started in 2003 with Kate being one of William's university flatmates. The couple got so much attention from the media that William requested the paparazzi to give them more space and Kate complained of media harassment. In April 2007 they broke up, but a few months later in June they were already seen together again. Their engagement was published on 16th November 2010. Kate received the engagement ring of William's late mother Diana. They married in Westminster Abbey, a church where a lot of coronations and royal weddings were held, for example the wedding of George VI and the Queen Mum. Around 300 million people saw their wedding live on television. On 3rd December 2012 it was announced that Kate Middleton is pregnant.

Sources:

http://resources.woodlands-junior.kent.sch.uk/customs/questions/motto.html
Trip to the Westminster Abbey in 2007
http://en.wikipedia.org/wiki/Coronation_of_the_British_monarch
http://www.britroyals.com/kings.asp?id=offa
http://www.britroyals.com/kings.asp?id=william1
"The Tudors" – TV series by Showtime
http://en.wikipedia.org/wiki/Henry_VIII_of_England
http://en.wikipedia.org/wiki/Elizabeth_II
http://en.wikipedia.org/wiki/Wedding_of_Prince_William_and_Catherine_Middleton